WORKBOOK

FOR

THE INNER WORK

An Invitation to True Freedom and Lasting Happiness

Zenful Work

Copyright

Disclaimer

This Companion Workbook to "THE INNER WORK " is an independent publication and is not an official companion guide to the book "THE INNER WORK" by Ashley Cottrell and Mathew Micheletti .It is not affiliated with or endorsed by the authors and is not intended to replace the main book. The purpose of this workbook is to offer additional insights, exercises, and activities to enhance your understanding and application of the concepts discussed in "THE INNER WORK" It is designed to be used as a supplementary tool for self-reflection, application, and personal growth, and not as a substitute for the original book.

This workbook

belongs to

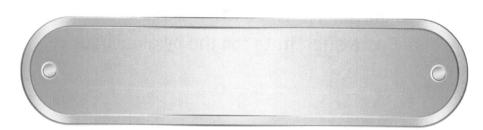

HOW TO USE THIS WORKBOOK

🪷 Read Mindfully: Begin by revisiting the corresponding chapter in "Peace Is Every Step." Absorb its teachings, allowing the words to resonate within you.

🪷 Engage Reflectively: Delve into the workbook's exercises and prompts. Reflect on your thoughts, feelings, and experiences as you respond to each activity.

🪷 Embrace Creativity: Use this workbook as a canvas for your innermost thoughts. Feel free to draw, write, or express yourself in any way that feels authentic.

🪷 Share and Connect: Consider discussing your insights with friends, family, or a supportive community. Sharing your journey can enhance your understanding and foster connections with others on a similar path.

🪷 Be Patient and Kind: Remember, self-discovery takes time. Be patient with yourself, and approach the activities with kindness and an open heart. Allow the process to unfold naturally.

PART I:
THE HUMAN EXPERIENCE

Chapter 1
Introduction to the inner work

This chapter introduces readers to the transformative journey of self-discovery, emphasizing the inherent potential for true freedom, lasting happiness, and inner peace within each individual. The authors stress that the path to these qualities lies in understanding and transcending the themes of consciousness that shape our experiences. It highlights the illusory nature of external pursuits for happiness and advocates for an internal shift in consciousness as the key to a fulfilling life.

POINTS TO REMEMBER

✓ Inherent Worthiness: Recognize your inherent worthiness for happiness, love, and freedom, irrespective of external circumstances.

✓ Consciousness Shapes Reality: Understand that your state of consciousness determines the quality of your experiences.

✓ Internal Transformation: True freedom and lasting happiness come from transforming your consciousness, not from external achievements.

✓ Self-Realization: The journey is a solo mission to realize your true self; only you can unlock the door to your happiness.

✓ Ongoing Choice: Life is a series of choices, and you are constantly choosing the life of your "not-self" or your true self.

 JOURNALLING PROMPTS

What does true freedom and lasting happiness mean to you?

_____

_____

_____

_____

_____

_____

_____

_____

_____

_____

_____

_____

_____

_____

_____

_____

_____

_____

_____

_____

_____

_____

_____

_____

JOURNALLING PROMPTS

Reflect on a moment when external achievements did not bring lasting joy. What insights can you draw?

_____

_____

_____

_____

_____

_____

_____

_____

_____

_____

_____

_____

_____

_____

_____

_____

_____

_____

_____

_____

_____

_____

 *JOURNALLING PROMPTS*

Explore a recurring challenge in your life. How might it be connected to a theme of consciousness?

_____

_____

_____

_____

_____

_____

_____

_____

_____

_____

_____

_____

_____

_____

_____

_____

_____

_____

_____

_____

_____

_____

 JOURNALLING PROMPTS

Consider instances where you felt truly happy. What was your state of mind at those moments?

JOURNALLING PROMPTS

Write about a dream life you've always imagined. How can internal transformation bring you closer to it?

JOURNALLING PROMPTS

In what ways do you see yourself choosing your "not-self" over your true self in daily life?

 JOURNALLING PROMPTS

Reflect on moments of inner peace. What themes of consciousness were prevalent during those times?

 JOURNALLING PROMPTS

Describe a situation where your consciousness played a significant role in your emotional experience.

_____
_____
_____
_____
_____
_____
_____
_____
_____
_____
_____
_____
_____
_____
_____
_____
_____
_____
_____
_____
_____
_____

 JOURNALLING PROMPTS

How do you currently perceive your worthiness for happiness and freedom?

_____
_____
_____
_____
_____
_____
_____
_____
_____
_____
_____
_____
_____
_____
_____
_____
_____
_____
_____
_____
_____
_____

 *JOURNALLING PROMPTS*

Imagine your life if you fully embraced your true self. What changes would you make?

_____

_____

_____

_____

_____

_____

_____

_____

_____

_____

_____

_____

_____

_____

_____

_____

_____

_____

_____

_____

_____

_____

_____

_____

ACTION PLANS

Consciousness Tracking

Throughout the week, observe your thoughts, emotions, and reactions. Note patterns and identify recurring themes.

Daily Affirmations

Create positive affirmations related to worthiness, love, and freedom. Repeat them daily to reinforce positive themes of consciousness.

Theme Transformation

Choose one limiting theme of consciousness you've identified and brainstorm ways to transform it into a liberating one.

Vision Board

Create a vision board that represents your true self and the life you desire. Display it in a visible place for daily inspiration.

Self-Reflective Questions

How do I currently define my worthiness for happiness and love?

What external pursuits have I believed would bring me lasting happiness?

How do I respond to challenges, and what themes of consciousness dominate these responses?

In what areas of my life do I feel the need for true freedom and lasting happiness?

What limiting beliefs about myself may be hindering my journey toward inner peace?

THOUGHTS AND REFLECTIONS

THOUGHTS AND REFLECTIONS

Chapter 2
Compassion for Ourselves and Others
Along the Journey

The authors encourage readers to recognize that their current perspectives, if not rooted in unconditional love, are subjective and temporary. The true self is described as perfect, loving awareness, and the potential for greatness is portrayed as pure innocence and joy. Affirmations are provided to challenge and shift limiting beliefs, promoting self-honesty as the first step in revealing one's current theme of consciousness. The chapter explores the mind's resistance to positive affirmations, highlighting the need to release and replace root program beliefs hindering the experience of love, peace, and happiness.

POINTS TO REMEMBER

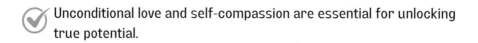

✓ Unconditional love and self-compassion are essential for unlocking true potential.

✓ Affirmations can be powerful tools to challenge and change limiting beliefs.

✓ The mind's resistance indicates limitations it imposes on one's experience of reality.

✓ Happiness is an internal commitment unrelated to external circumstances.

✓ Acceptance, surrender, and humble allowance are integral to the process of inner work.

 JOURNALLING PROMPTS

How did you feel while reading the affirmations? Note any discomfort or resistance.

_____

_____

_____

_____

_____

_____

_____

_____

_____

_____

_____

_____

_____

_____

_____

_____

_____

_____

_____

_____

_____

_____

_____

_____

JOURNALLING PROMPTS

Identify affirmations that triggered a strong reaction and explore the associated thoughts.

_____
_____
_____
_____
_____
_____
_____
_____
_____
_____
_____
_____
_____
_____
_____
_____
_____
_____
_____
_____
_____

⚘ JOURNALLING PROMPTS ⚘

Reflect on the mind's defense mechanisms against positive affirmations. What does it reveal about your current theme of consciousness?

JOURNALLING PROMPTS

Examine any rationalizations or excuses your mind presents for resisting happiness and self-love.

_____
_____
_____
_____
_____
_____
_____
_____
_____
_____
_____
_____
_____
_____
_____
_____
_____
_____
_____
_____
_____
_____
_____
_____

Write down moments in your life where you've felt genuine joy, love, or peace. What themes or patterns do you notice?

# JOURNALLING PROMPTS

Explore moments in your life when you felt fully accepted and loved. What contributed to those feelings, and how can you recreate such experiences?

 JOURNALLING PROMPTS

Consider the affirmations that made you cringe. What specific beliefs or past experiences might be influencing your discomfort?

JOURNALLING PROMPTS

Reflect on the concept of self-forgiveness. Are there past actions or mistakes you struggle to forgive yourself for? How might self-forgiveness impact your well-being?

_____

_____

_____

_____

_____

_____

_____

_____

_____

_____

_____

_____

_____

_____

_____

_____

_____

_____

_____

_____

_____

_____

_____

_____

_____

_____

Identify situations where you've faced fears with courage in the past. What strengths or qualities did you draw upon, and how can you apply them to current challenges?

_____

_____

_____

_____

_____

_____

_____

_____

_____

_____

_____

_____

_____

_____

_____

_____

_____

_____

_____

_____

_____

_____

_____

_____

❀ JOURNALLING PROMPTS ❀

Imagine a future where you fully embrace self-love and unconditional acceptance. What changes do you foresee in your thoughts, actions, and overall well-being?

ACTION PLANS

Daily Affirmation Practice

Commit to reciting positive affirmations daily, observing your reactions and noting any changes in perspective.

Affirmation Reversal

Take a limiting belief and create a positive affirmation to counteract it. Repeat the new affirmation regularly.

Gratitude Journal

List three things you're grateful for each day, focusing on cultivating a positive mindset.

Compassionate Self-Talk

Replace self-critical thoughts with compassionate and encouraging language throughout the day.

How do I currently define my self-worth, and is it rooted in unconditional love?

What fears or resistances arise when considering the potential for unconditional self-love?

How willing am I to release old narratives and beliefs that no longer serve my well-being?

What role does self-compassion play in my daily interactions with myself and others?

THOUGHTS AND REFLECTIONS

THOUGHTS AND REFLECTIONS

Chapter 3
The Human Plight

"The Human Plight" delves into the common human tendency to project happiness onto future events or achievements, creating a mindset that life will be better when certain conditions are met. It emphasizes that the key to true happiness lies in the present moment, not in some future destination. The chapter explores the limiting beliefs and themes that hinder personal growth and happiness, focusing on the ego's role in creating mental programs and attachments. It introduces the concept of Inner Work as a means of breaking free from limiting themes and rediscovering one's true self.

POINTS TO REMEMBER

✓ Happiness is in the Now: It is important to find joy and contentment in the present moment rather than relying on future events for fulfillment.

✓ The Power of Inner Work: Inner Work involves recognizing and challenging limiting beliefs, thoughts, and emotions that hinder personal growth. It's a journey toward self-realization and liberation.

✓ Attachment to Ego: The ego creates mental programs and attachments to past traumas, judgments, and expectations, blocking the experience of joy and peace. Recognizing and letting go of these attachments is essential for personal freedom.

✓ True Identity: The chapter explores the formation of the ego persona, emphasizing that beneath the layers of experiences, one's true identity is innocent, free, and inherently blissful.

✓ Surrender and Freedom: Surrendering to the present moment and the Divine Will is a powerful demonstration of inner freedom. Letting go of the ego's need for control leads to lasting happiness.

Reflect on a specific future event or achievement you associate with happiness. How can you find joy in the present while working towards that goal?

☙ JOURNALLING PROMPTS ☙

Identify areas in your life where you deny yourself happiness through past trauma, self-consciousness, fault-finding, hopelessness, or other limiting beliefs.

_____

_____

_____

_____

_____

_____

_____

_____

_____

_____

_____

_____

_____

_____

_____

_____

_____

_____

_____

_____

_____

_____

_____

_____

_____

_____

❀ JOURNALLING PROMPTS ❀

Consider moments when you've felt truly free and joyful. What were the circumstances, and how can you bring more of those elements into your daily life?

Explore your ego's attachments. What past experiences or identities do you cling to, and how do they impact your present well-being?

❧ JOURNALLING PROMPTS ❧

Imagine yourself as the five-year-old mentioned in the chapter. What layers have you added to protect yourself, and how might removing them reveal your true, blissful self?

_____

_____

_____

_____

_____

_____

_____

_____

_____

_____

_____

_____

_____

_____

_____

_____

_____

_____

_____

_____

_____

_____

JOURNALLING PROMPTS

How does the constant chatter of your mind affect your daily experiences? Can you identify moments when you're not fully present due to inner dialogue?

_____

_____

_____

_____

_____

_____

_____

_____

_____

_____

_____

_____

_____

_____

_____

_____

_____

_____

_____

_____

_____

_____

_____

_____

☙ JOURNALLING PROMPTS ☙

Reflect on the concept of surrender. In what areas of your life can you practice letting go of control and trusting in a higher power or the natural flow of life?

Consider times when external circumstances significantly influenced your mood. How might your perspective change if you detached your inner experience from external events?

_____

_____

_____

_____

_____

_____

_____

_____

_____

_____

_____

_____

_____

_____

_____

_____

_____

_____

_____

_____

_____

_____

_____

❧ JOURNALLING PROMPTS ❧

Explore the idea of self-realization. What aspects of your identity are based on societal conditioning or external influences, and how can you reconnect with your true self?

☙ JOURNALLING PROMPTS ☙

Contemplate the quote, "It is better to conquer yourself than to win a thousand battles." How can self-awareness and inner transformation lead to lasting victories in your life?

ACTION PLANS

Mindfulness Meditation

Practice five minutes of daily mindfulness meditation to observe your thoughts without attachment. Focus on your breath and cultivate awareness of the present moment.

Nature Connection

Observe the beauty around you, and reflect on the interconnectedness of all life. Nature can be a powerful teacher of presence and surrender.

Ego Detox

Choose a day to consciously observe and challenge your ego's reactions. When faced with challenges, ask yourself, "Is this a reaction of my true self or my ego?"

Inner Child Visualization

Engage in a visualization exercise where you reconnect with your inner child. Imagine peeling away layers of protective blankets to reveal your true, innocent self.

How does my mindset about future happiness impact my current well-being?

What recurring thoughts or beliefs limit my ability to experience joy and freedom in the present?

In what areas of my life do I find it challenging to let go of control and surrender to the natural flow?

How can I differentiate between my true self and the ego persona in various situations?

What practices or habits can I incorporate into my daily life to enhance self-awareness and break free from limiting themes?

THOUGHTS AND REFLECTIONS

THOUGHTS AND REFLECTIONS

PART II: LIBERATION FROM THE MIND

Chapter 4
Meet Your Mind

In this chapter, emphasis lies in the crucial realization that we are not our thoughts. The chapter guides readers to observe their inner dialogue as impartial observers, revealing the themes of consciousness and prompting a shift in awareness. The resistance from the ego-mind is acknowledged, described as a natural part of the awakening process. It delves into how our thoughts are shaped by early experiences and societal influences, creating themes of consciousness that dictate our perceptions and behaviors. The concept of the mind as an innocent machine is introduced, highlighting its tendency to defend itself through projection and distraction. The chapter encourages readers to become watchers of their thoughts, fostering awareness and compassion in the journey toward self-discovery and liberation.

POINTS TO REMEMBER

✓ You Are Not Your Thoughts: Recognize that your thoughts do not define you, and challenging them is essential for true freedom.

✓ Resistance is Natural: Understand that the mind's resistance to change is born out of ignorance, not malice, and viewing it with compassion is crucial.

✓ Question Inherited Beliefs: Many thoughts and beliefs are inherited or modeled; question them to discover your true self beyond societal influences.

✓ Break the Cycle: Recognize and break the cycles of negative thoughts and emotions that have become ingrained through repetition.

✓ Awareness Leads to Freedom: By becoming aware of your thoughts, you can break free from subconscious patterns and choose more positive responses to life.

JOURNALLING PROMPTS

What are the dominant themes in your inner dialogue?

_____
_____
_____
_____
_____
_____
_____
_____
_____
_____
_____
_____
_____
_____
_____
_____
_____
_____
_____
_____
_____
_____
_____
_____

❧ JOURNALLING PROMPTS ❧

How have societal influences shaped your beliefs and thoughts?

# JOURNALLING PROMPTS

What inherited beliefs or thought patterns do you want to challenge or change?

🪷 JOURNALLING PROMPTS 🪷

Are you feeding the "good wolf" or the "evil wolf" in your mental narratives?

_____
_____
_____
_____
_____
_____
_____
_____
_____
_____
_____
_____
_____
_____
_____
_____
_____
_____
_____
_____
_____

What would your be without the influence of inherited thoughts and beliefs?

_____

_____

_____

_____

_____

_____

_____

_____

_____

_____

_____

_____

_____

_____

_____

_____

_____

_____

_____

_____

_____

✲ JOURNALLING PROMPTS ✲

How does resistance manifest in your mind, and how can you view it with compassion?

_____

_____

_____

_____

_____

_____

_____

_____

_____

_____

_____

_____

_____

_____

_____

_____

_____

_____

_____

_____

_____

JOURNALLING PROMPTS

Identify a recurring negative thought and explore its origins and validity.

JOURNALLING PROMPTS

In what ways do your project blame onto external factors for your inner struggles?

_____

_____

_____

_____

_____

_____

_____

_____

_____

_____

_____

_____

_____

_____

_____

_____

_____

_____

_____

_____

_____

_____

_____

_____

 *JOURNALLING PROMPTS*

Describe a moment when you broke free from a negative thought pattern; how did it feel?

 JOURNALLING PROMPTS

Reflect on a positive theme of consciousness you want to cultivate; what steps can you take?

_____

_____

_____

_____

_____

_____

_____

_____

_____

_____

_____

_____

_____

_____

_____

_____

_____

_____

_____

_____

_____

_____

ACTION PLANS

Mindfulness Meditation

Practice observing your thoughts without judgment during a short mindfulness meditation daily.

Thought Pattern Tracker

Create a log to track recurring thought patterns, noting their emotional impact and identifying triggers.

Theme of Consciousness Art

Express your dominant theme of consciousness through art or writing, allowing for creative exploration.

Positive Affirmations

Develop and recite positive affirmations daily to counteract negative thought patterns.

Self-Reflective Questions

How does my understanding of the mind as an innocent machine influence my self-compassion?

What role does resistance play in my personal growth, and how can I navigate it more effectively?

In what areas of my life do I see the strongest influence of inherited beliefs, and how do they impact my well-being?

How can I bring more awareness to my thought patterns without judgment?

What steps can I take to break free from a particularly limiting theme of consciousness?

THOUGHTS AND REFLECTIONS

THOUGHTS AND REFLECTIONS

Chapter 5
Anatomy of Thoughts and The Beneficial Use of Mind

Summary

Here, we explore the anatomy of a thought and the beneficial use of the mind. It emphasizes the idea that everything is energy and highlights the role of consciousness in shaping reality. The chapter discusses the importance of tuning into the right frequency of thought, being receptive to inspiration, and the transformative power of silence. It encourages readers to be aware of the themes of consciousness they are tuned into and to consciously choose positive frequencies for a more fulfilling life.

POINTS TO REMEMBER

✓ Conscious Tuning: Your mind is like a radio, and your consciousness determines the thoughts you receive. Consciously choose the frequency you want to tune into.

✓ Silent Receptivity: True inspiration arises in moments of silence. Cultivate a surrendered, silent mind to receive genuine insights and creativity effortlessly.

✓ Power of Awareness: Recognize the themes of consciousness you engage with. Awareness is the first step toward reclaiming the power to consciously respond to situations.

✓ Mind and Ego: Distinguish between the mind, a receiver of inspiration, and the ego, which seeks credit. Practice humility in acknowledging inspired thoughts.

✓ Emotional Guidance: Emotions indicate the frequency of consciousness. Use emotions as a guide to understand the themes you are tuned into and consciously choose your responses.

⚘ JOURNALLING PROMPTS ⚘

Reflect on a moment when you experienced genuine inspiration. What themes of consciousness were prevalent at that time?

_____

_____

_____

_____

_____

_____

_____

_____

_____

_____

_____

_____

_____

_____

_____

_____

_____

_____

_____

_____

_____

_____

_____

☙ JOURNALLING PROMPTS ❧

Describe the impact of silence on your mind. How comfortable are you with moments of mental stillness?

✿ JOURNALLING PROMPTS ✿

Explore a recent situation where your reaction was unconscious. What theme of consciousness were you aligned with, and how could you have consciously responded?

☙ JOURNALLING PROMPTS ☙

List three recurring thoughts that dominate your mind. Are they aligned with the frequencies you wish to experience?

❧ JOURNALLING PROMPTS ❧

Consider a challenging situation. How might consciously choosing a different frequency of thought have altered your experience?

_____

_____

_____

_____

_____

_____

_____

_____

_____

_____

_____

_____

_____

_____

_____

_____

_____

_____

_____

_____

_____

_____

_____

☙ JOURNALLING PROMPTS ☙

Write about the role of ego in your thought processes.
How can you cultivate humility in acknowledging the
source of your thoughts?

Describe a moment when you felt a deep sense of inner peace. What themes of consciousness were present, and how can you invite more of these into your life?

_____

_____

_____

_____

_____

_____

_____

_____

_____

_____

_____

_____

_____

_____

_____

_____

_____

_____

_____

_____

_____

_____

_____

 JOURNALLING PROMPTS

Explore the concept of "flow state." When do you usually experience it, and what conditions contribute to its emergence?

_____

_____

_____

_____

_____

_____

_____

_____

_____

_____

_____

_____

_____

_____

_____

_____

_____

_____

_____

_____

_____

_____

_____

_____

_____

 JOURNALLING PROMPTS

How do you currently deal with moments of silence in your mind? Are there fears or resistance associated with mental stillness?

_____

_____

_____

_____

_____

_____

_____

_____

_____

_____

_____

_____

_____

_____

_____

_____

_____

_____

_____

_____

_____

_____

_____

☙ JOURNALLING PROMPTS ❧

Reflect on a recent emotional reaction. What songs were playing on the "station" of your consciousness at that moment?

ACTION PLANS

Conscious Theme Selection

Throughout the day, consciously choose the theme of consciousness you want to engage with. Notice how it affects your thoughts and emotions.

Inspired Gratitude Journal

Create a journal specifically for recording inspired thoughts. Express gratitude for each one, recognizing them as gifts from the infinite field of consciousness.

Ego-Release Practice

Identify one thought or idea you usually attribute to your ego. Practice releasing attachment to it and acknowledging it as part of the collective consciousness.

Emotional Frequency Check

Regularly check in with your emotions. If you find yourself in a negative emotional state, consciously shift to a more positive frequency by engaging in activities that bring joy.

How can I create more mental spaciousness in my daily life to invite genuine inspiration?

In what ways do societal beliefs influence the themes of consciousness i tune into?

What role does humility play in my relationship with inspired thoughts?

Are there specific environments or situations that consistently tune me into negative frequencies?

THOUGHTS AND REFLECTIONS

THOUGHTS AND REFLECTIONS

Chapter 6
Presence and Awareness of The Observer

This delves into the concepts of presence and awareness of the observer. It emphasizes the practice of watching the mind's constant chatter, leading to a sense of separation from ego-driven thoughts. Awareness is presented as a tool for breaking free from the patterns of limiting consciousness, allowing individuals to choose their responses consciously. The chapter explores the profound shift that occurs when one becomes aware of their mental patterns and the empowering nature of this realization. Presence, transcending the mind's noise, is introduced as a state where life is experienced in slow motion, appreciating every detail without distraction. The authors conclude by highlighting the implications of reclaiming presence, acknowledging the challenges in staying present, and the transformative power of continuous inner work

POINTS TO REMEMBER

✓ Awareness Breaks Patterns: Awareness of the mind's chatter enables a separation from ego-driven thoughts, allowing conscious choice of themes of consciousness.

✓ Empowerment through Awareness: Recognizing mental patterns is empowering, akin to waking up from a state of unaware imprisonment. It allows for lasting change and compassion towards oneself.

✓ Presence Transcends Mind Noise: Presence goes beyond the mind's noise, providing a slow-motion experience of life where every detail is appreciated without distraction.

✓ Gratitude and Presence: Gratitude is a powerful tool to evoke presence, eliminating suffering and fostering acceptance. Shifting the inner narrative to gratitude can be done at will.

✓ Meditation for Awareness: Meditation, as a tool for watching the mind, strengthens awareness and facilitates the practice of presence. Impersonal observation of thoughts is emphasized.

☙ JOURNALLING PROMPTS ☙

Reflect on a moment when awareness allowed you to choose a different response to a situation. How did this impact the outcome?

❀ JOURNALLING PROMPTS ❀

Describe a moment when you realized the collective nature of your existence, connecting you to your ancestors and the broader community.

JOURNALLING PROMPTS

Share a personal experience of borrowing mindfulness from others to overcome a challenging situation. How did their support impact your well-being?

_____

_____

_____

_____

_____

_____

_____

_____

_____

_____

_____

_____

_____

_____

_____

_____

_____

_____

_____

_____

_____

Explore the concept of presence. Can you recall a specific instance when you experienced life in slow motion, appreciating every detail?

_____

_____

_____

_____

_____

_____

_____

_____

_____

_____

_____

_____

_____

_____

_____

_____

_____

_____

_____

_____

_____

_____

_____

❀ JOURNALLING PROMPTS ❀

Consider a situation where you felt imprisoned by your thoughts before becoming aware. How did awareness change your perspective?

_____
_____
_____
_____
_____
_____
_____
_____
_____
_____
_____
_____
_____
_____
_____
_____
_____
_____
_____
_____
_____
_____
_____
_____

JOURNALLING PROMPTS

Describe a mundane moment where practicing gratitude shifted your inner narrative. What details did you appreciate in that moment?

JOURNALLING PROMPTS

Reflect on the implications of staying present in daily life. How does it affect your perception of yourself and others?

☸ JOURNALLING PROMPTS ☸

Write about the challenges you face in maintaining awareness amidst the mind's constant chatter. How do distractions impact your ability to stay present?

✿ JOURNALLING PROMPTS ✿

Explore the idea of meditation as a tool for awareness. How has formal meditation or mindfulness practices influenced your ability to stay present?

☙ JOURNALLING PROMPTS ☙

Recall a moment of witnessing the mind's chatter without attachment. How did this experience contribute to your understanding of thoughts?

☙ JOURNALLING PROMPTS ❧

Write about the role of acceptance in evoking presence. How does acceptance of the present moment contribute to a sense of inner peace

_____

_____

_____

_____

_____

_____

_____

_____

_____

_____

_____

_____

_____

_____

_____

_____

_____

_____

_____

_____

_____

_____

 JOURNALLING PROMPTS

Reflect on the transformative power of continuous inner work. How have small, mundane moments become opportunities for breakthroughs in your life?

_____

_____

_____

_____

_____

_____

_____

_____

_____

_____

_____

_____

_____

_____

_____

_____

_____

_____

_____

_____

_____

_____

_____

ACTION PLANS

Presence Moments

Throughout the day, take intentional moments to shift your focus to the present. Notice and appreciate the details of your surroundings.

Mindfulness Meditation

Set aside time for daily meditation, focusing on watching the mind without attachment. Gradually increase the duration of your meditation sessions.

Awareness Check-ins

Periodically check in with your awareness throughout the day. Ask yourself, "What theme of consciousness am I currently tuned into?"

Acceptance Practice

In challenging situations, practice acceptance of the present moment. Explore how this shifts your response and overall experience.

In what ways does gratitude contribute to my experience of presence?

How do distractions impact my ability to stay present?

What strategies can I employ to minimize distractions and enhance my awareness?

THOUGHTS AND REFLECTIONS

THOUGHTS AND REFLECTIONS

PART III:

LIBERATION OF CONSCIOUSNESS

Chapter 7
Presence and Awareness of The Observer

Summary

The authors introduce various themes, ranging from true freedom and lasting happiness to negative themes such as fear, anger, and shame. Using awareness, the chapter emphasizes how these themes influence every aspect of life, coloring perceptions and shaping responses to situations. The authors draw parallels with Dr. Masaru Emoto's experiments on water crystals to illustrate how vibrational frequencies associated with different themes affect the physical realm. The chapter delves into the viewpoints and experiences associated with each theme, providing examples related to debt and credit. It concludes by highlighting the interconnectedness of themes of consciousness and the potential for change through Inner Work

POINTS TO REMEMBER

✓ Influence of Themes: Themes of consciousness deeply influence thoughts, feelings, and actions, shaping individual experiences and perspectives.

✓ Water Crystal Analogy: The experiments of Dr. Masaru Emoto illustrate how vibrational frequencies associated with themes manifest visually, emphasizing the tangible impact of consciousness.

✓ Perspectives on Debt and Credit: Examples demonstrate how different themes of consciousness perceive and react to situations, such as debt and credit.

✓ Interconnectedness of Themes: Each theme of consciousness is interconnected with various aspects of life, including thoughts, feelings, desires, habits, and interests.

✓ Freedom and Happiness Choice: True freedom and lasting happiness are presented as continuous lifestyle choices that transcend limiting themes of consciousness, requiring conscious awareness and surrender.

☙ JOURNALLING PROMPTS ❧

Reflect on a situation where you observed the influence of a specific theme of consciousness on your thoughts, feelings, and actions. How did it shape your experience?

⚘ *JOURNALLING PROMPTS* ⚘

Consider the examples related to debt and credit in the chapter. How does your current perspective on financial matters align with or differ from the themes discussed?

🪷 JOURNALLING PROMPTS 🪷

Explore a moment when you felt a shift in your vibrational frequency, akin to the water crystal experiments. What theme of consciousness were you embodying, and how did it impact your experience?

❀ JOURNALLING PROMPTS ❀

Identify recurring patterns in your life and connect them to themes of consciousness. Are there specific themes that dominate certain aspects of your life?

_____

_____

_____

_____

_____

_____

_____

_____

_____

_____

_____

_____

_____

_____

_____

_____

_____

_____

_____

_____

_____

_____

_____

 JOURNALLING PROMPTS

Reflect on the interconnectedness of themes in your experiences. How does your theme of consciousness in one area of life influence other areas?

❧ JOURNALLING PROMPTS ❧

Contemplate the idea that true freedom and lasting happiness are continuous lifestyle choices. How can you integrate this awareness into your daily life?

☙ JOURNALLING PROMPTS ❧

Consider the role of negativity and dissatisfaction in your life. How has your ego convinced you of a payoff in maintaining negative beliefs?

# JOURNALLING PROMPTS

Explore the concept of addiction to stress, suffering, or victimization. In what ways have your body and brain become accustomed to certain emotional patterns?

❀ JOURNALLING PROMPTS ❀

Reflect on the possibility of change. How can consistent Inner Work contribute to rewiring your brain's neurochemistry and shifting your themes of consciousness ?

# JOURNALLING PROMPTS

Contemplate the ultimate choice present in every moment. How can you make choices that align with themes of consciousness that bring happiness and inner peace?

ACTION PLANS

Theme Identification

Spend time identifying the dominant theme of consciousness in specific areas of your life. Journal about how this theme influences your thoughts and actions.

Water Crystal Visualization

Use visualization techniques to imagine the vibrational frequencies associated with different themes impacting the water within your body. Observe how this visualization affects your overall energy.

Debt and Credit Reflection

Reflect on your attitudes towards debt and credit. How does your perspective align with or differ from the examples provided in the chapter?

Daily Theme Check-ins

Throughout the day, pause and check in with your current theme of consciousness. How does it influence your reactions to different situations?

How have I observed themes of consciousness influencing my daily life, including thoughts, feelings, and actions?

How do I react to the idea that true freedom and lasting happiness are continuous lifestyle choices?

What changes can I make to align more closely with these choices?

THOUGHTS AND REFLECTIONS

THOUGHTS AND REFLECTIONS

Chapter 8
Practicing the Inner Work

Chapter 8 of "Inner Work" delves into the practical application of The Inner Work philosophy. The chapter underscores the importance of using awareness, personal responsibility, and inner work to transform unskillful reactions into balanced responses. The central aim is to realign oneself with love and joy in every moment, thus living in an awakened state as the true Self.

POINTS TO REMEMBER

✅ Awareness is the First Step: Recognizing triggers and acknowledging internal reactions is the initial key to transformation.

✅ Root Program Identification: Understanding the root program beliefs behind triggers provides insight into one's unconscious patterns.

✅ Conscious Choice: The pause between a trigger and response is a space for conscious choice and the opportunity to rewrite the narrative.

✅ Small Moments Lead to Lasting Shifts: Genuine healing and change come from consistent, small moments of choosing new narratives over inherited programs.

✅ Transformation is Continuous: The Inner Work is a contemplative practice applicable in everyday moments, leading to ongoing evolution and adaptation.

 JOURNALLING PROMPTS

Reflect on recent moments of discomfort or disturbance.
What triggered these reactions?

 JOURNALLING PROMPTS

For each trigger identified, delve into the underlying beliefs. What patterns or themes emerge?

✿ JOURNALLING PROMPTS ✿

Imagine an alternative, positive narrative for each trigger.
How does this shift in perspective feel?

 JOURNALLING PROMPTS

Are there commonalities among triggers? Do they reveal recurring themes in your life?

☙ JOURNALLING PROMPTS ❧

Journal about instances where choosing a new narrative led to a tangible shift in your emotions or action

✿ JOURNALLING PROMPTS ✿

Describe a small, everyday situation where you consciously chose a new narrative. How did it contribute to your overall well-being?

✤ JOURNALLING PROMPTS ✤

Explore how Inner Work can positively influence your interactions with others. Share an example.

🪷 JOURNALLING PROMPTS 🪷

What new narratives do you want to consciously cultivate
in your life moving forward?

_____

_____

_____

_____

_____

_____

_____

_____

_____

_____

_____

_____

_____

_____

_____

_____

_____

_____

_____

_____

_____

_____

❀ JOURNALLING PROMPTS ❀

Reflect on instances where you've noticed a change in your responses. How can you celebrate these small victories?

 JOURNALLING PROMPTS

Consider how Inner Work aligns with your existing beliefs and values. How can you integrate it into your daily routine?

_____

_____

_____

_____

_____

_____

_____

_____

_____

_____

_____

_____

_____

_____

_____

_____

_____

_____

_____

_____

_____

_____

ACTION PLANS

Mindful Trigger Observation

Pick a day to mindfully observe your reactions to triggers without judgment. Take notes on the triggers and your initial responses.

Role Play Exercise

Enlist a friend or family member to engage in role play scenarios that typically trigger you. Practice choosing new narratives in these scenarios

Daily Trigger Log

Create a daily log to track triggers, associated root beliefs, and the chosen new narrative. Review at the end of the week for patterns.

Guided Meditation

Incorporate a guided meditation focused on self-awareness and choosing new narratives into your daily routine.

How comfortable am I with acknowledging and examining my triggers?

In what ways do my root program beliefs influence my daily life and interactions?

How do I handle setbacks in the Inner Work process?

What role does self-compassion play in my journey of transformation?

THOUGHTS AND REFLECTIONS

THOUGHTS AND REFLECTIONS

Chapter 9
Healing The Wounded Themes of Consciousness

Summary

This focuses on the exploration and transcendence of limiting themes of consciousness. These themes, such as pride, anger, desire, fear, grief, hopelessness, guilt, judgment, and shame, are discussed as layers of resistance to accepting one's true nature of unconditional love. The chapter emphasizes that while experiencing these themes is a natural part of being human, suffering arises when one becomes attached and stuck in them.

It introduces the theme of shame, highlighting its roots in feelings of rejection and unworthiness. It discusses how shame can manifest in various forms, from mild embarrassment to extreme self-loathing, and explores the impact of societal, familial, and religious influences on the development of shame. The narrative suggests that transcending shame involves recognizing its roots, understanding its projection, and embracing the truth of one's inherent innocence and unconditional love

POINTS TO REMEMBER

✓ Themes of Consciousness Progression: The limiting themes of consciousness represent layers of resistance, and individuals may find themselves more attached to certain themes than others.

✓ Innocence and Unconditional Love: Recognizing one's inherent innocence and understanding the unconditional love of God is crucial for transcending shame, guilt, and judgment.

✓ Consequence vs. Judgment: Distinguishing between consequence and judgment is essential for overcoming guilt. Accepting one's limitations and seeking humility is a path toward healing.

✓ Facing Loss and Seeking Help: Hopelessness can be transcended by allowing oneself to feel, facing the emotions of grief, and seeking support from others or a Higher Power.

✓ Transcendence Requires Curiosity: Inviting curiosity and seeking guidance are essential steps in transcending limiting themes. Accepting help and allowing oneself to ask for assistance are signs of strength.

❀ JOURNALLING PROMPTS ❀

Recall instances in your life where you felt shame. Explore the triggers, root beliefs, and the impact of societal or familial influences on these experiences.

❧ JOURNALLING PROMPTS ❧

Reflect on times when you experienced guilt. Identify the perceived mistakes, the root program beliefs, and the difference between healthy acknowledgment and destructive guilt.

❧ JOURNALLING PROMPTS ❧

Consider situations in your life that triggered feelings of hopelessness. Examine the root beliefs associated with these emotions and how they might be connected to past traumas or losses.

☙ JOURNALLING PROMPTS ☙

Write about moments in your life when you felt innocent and loved. How can you carry this awareness into challenging situations?

_____

_____

_____

_____

_____

_____

_____

_____

_____

_____

_____

_____

_____

_____

_____

_____

_____

_____

_____

_____

_____

❁ JOURNALLING PROMPTS ❁

Embrace curiosity about your limiting themes. Ask yourself: What can I learn from these experiences? How can I grow through them?

_____
_____
_____
_____
_____
_____
_____
_____
_____
_____
_____
_____
_____
_____
_____
_____
_____
_____
_____
_____
_____
_____
_____
_____
_____

 JOURNALLING PROMPTS

Evaluate your current support system. Who can you turn
to for help or guidance when facing challenging emotions?

_____

_____

_____

_____

_____

_____

_____

_____

_____

_____

_____

_____

_____

_____

_____

_____

_____

_____

_____

_____

_____

_____

_____

_____

🪷 JOURNALLING PROMPTS 🪷

Reflect on instances where humility played a role in overcoming judgment. How did it shift your perspective?

✿ JOURNALLING PROMPTS ✿

Consider a significant loss in your life. How have you coped with it, and what emotions have you allowed yourself to feel or suppress?

JOURNALLING PROMPTS

Share an experience where making a mistake led to significant personal growth. What lessons did you learn?

 JOURNALLING PROMPTS

If you're currently facing challenges, write a letter to yourself asking for help and guidance. What support would you like to receive ?

ACTION PLANS

Meditative Reflection

Practice a guided meditation focused on recognizing your inherent innocence and reconnecting with the unconditional love of God.

Symbolic Release

Create a symbolic representation of shame, guilt, or hopelessness, and ceremoniously release it as a gesture of letting go.

Support Network Building

Identify individuals in your life whom you can turn to for support during challenging times. Strengthen those connections through communication

Grief Journaling

Start a grief journal to explore and express emotions associated with loss. Allow yourself to feel and acknowledge the impact of these losses on your life.

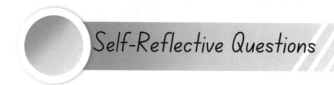

What role does unconditional love play in my understanding of innocence and self-worth?

In what ways can humility be a catalyst for overcoming judgment and guilt in my life?

How comfortable am I with seeking help and support from others or a Higher Power when facing challenging emotions?

THOUGHTS AND REFLECTIONS

THOUGHTS AND REFLECTIONS

PART IV :
A NEW PARADIGM

Chapter 10
Accepting Our Destiny

The chapter emphasizes the theme of courage as the key to growth and the gateway to higher dimensions of consciousness. The chapter explores the evolution of consciousness through liberating themes, focusing on true freedom, lasting happiness, love, inner peace, reason, understanding, acceptance, willingness, and neutrality. Courage, represented by the archetype of the Honorable Warrior, signifies the transition into self-honesty, moral responsibility, and the acknowledgment of one's insecurities.

The chapter encourages readers to move beyond the need for battles and confrontations, ultimately reaching a state of neutrality before progressing further." the authors explore the evolution of consciousness, focusing on the interplay between reason, understanding, and spiritual transcendence. The narrative emphasizes that a shift from a purely objective, reasoning mind to a more subjective, spiritually aware perspective is essential for personal growth and a deeper understanding of existence.

POINTS TO REMEMBER

- Courage as Empowerment: Courage marks the shift from resisting life to embracing it, affirming love, and accessing true power.

- Self-Honesty and Integrity: The theme of courage involves facing ego insecurities, admitting fears, and choosing good over evil, leading to self-accountability.

- Transcending Confrontation: Moving through courage requires surrendering the need to fight, realizing that true peace comes from non-participation.

- Balancing Reason and Spirituality: Recognize the importance of integrating reason and understanding with spiritual awareness for a comprehensive understanding of life.

- Transcending Ego: Overcome the ego's attachment to pride and vanity by acknowledging that true genius and understanding come through us, not from us.

- Consciousness Influences Perception: Understand that consciousness shapes our perception of the external world, and subjective spiritual realities play a vital role in determining our quality of life

JOURNALLING PROMPTS

Reflect on a recent situation where you demonstrated courage. How did it feel to face your fears or insecurities?

⚜ JOURNALLING PROMPTS ⚜

Describe a moment when you found yourself in a state of neutrality. What brought about the feeling of non-confrontation and rest?

_____

_____

_____

_____

_____

_____

_____

_____

_____

_____

_____

_____

_____

_____

_____

_____

_____

_____

_____

_____

_____

_____

 # JOURNALLING PROMPTS

Explore your aspirations and what drives you. How does willingness manifest in your life, and what goals are you motivated to achieve?

 JOURNALLING PROMPTS

Consider a situation where acceptance played a crucial role. How did accepting the circumstances impact your emotional well-being?

☙ JOURNALLING PROMPTS ❧

Dive into your journey of reason and understanding. What areas of knowledge or understanding are you currently exploring, and why?

_____

_____

_____

_____

_____

_____

_____

_____

_____

_____

_____

_____

_____

_____

_____

_____

_____

_____

_____

_____

_____

_____

_____

☙ JOURNALLING PROMPTS ❧

Investigate your attachment to specific thoughts as "mine." How might detaching from these thoughts contribute to a more open and receptive mind?

_____

_____

_____

_____

_____

_____

_____

_____

_____

_____

_____

_____

_____

_____

_____

_____

_____

_____

_____

_____

_____

_____

_____

_____

JOURNALLING PROMPTS

Reflect on instances when you've felt a deep connection to a spiritual reality beyond your immediate perception. How can you cultivate and deepen this connection?

☙ JOURNALLING PROMPTS ☙

Explore a challenging question about existence, such as "Who am I?" or "What is the purpose of my life?" Reflect on your current understanding and any shifts in perspective.

☙ JOURNALLING PROMPTS ☙

Write about a belief or faith that you hold but can't
objectively prove. How does this belief contribute to your
overall well-being?

❀ JOURNALLING PROMPTS ❀

Describe a personal experience where your consciousness influenced your perception of reality. How did this realization impact your subsequent actions and choices?

 *JOURNALLING PROMPTS*

Explore the concept of love as the most logical choice. How can you embody and express love in your daily life, considering both personal relationships and interactions with the broader world?

ACTION PLANS

Courageous Affirmations

Create a list of affirmations that resonate with the energy of courage. Repeat them daily to reinforce your commitment to facing challenges with bravery.

Neutrality Meditation

Practice a meditation focused on letting go of the need to confront or change things. Embrace neutrality and observe the peace that arises.

Acceptance Practice

Choose a situation that challenges you and consciously practice accepting it without judgment. Note how this shifts your emotional state.

Spiritual Exploration

Attend a spiritual or philosophical discussion group to explore different perspectives on existence. Engage in open-minded dialogue and observe the impact on your beliefs.

Self-Reflective Questions

How can I strike a balance between reason and spirituality in my daily life?

In what ways do my emotions influence my ability to objectively explore complex topics?

How can I cultivate a genuine sense of awe and gratitude for the knowledge I acquire?

What beliefs or faith do I hold that contribute positively to my well-being?

How can I contribute my knowledge and skills for the betterment of humanity, devoid of ego and pride?

THOUGHTS AND REFLECTIONS

THOUGHTS AND REFLECTIONS

Chapter 11
True Freedom and Lasting Happiness

Summary

Here we look into the concept of true freedom and lasting happiness, emphasizing the role of faith and spirituality in transcending the limitations of reason and understanding. The chapter explores the shift from relying solely on reason to embracing spiritual reality, where consciousness is acknowledged as the source of identity. It discusses the power of belief and faith, exemplified by the placebo effect, and how consciousness, as the true Self, is beyond time and space.

The narrative underscores that true freedom and lasting happiness come from accepting a spiritual context of reality. The ego's attachment to the physical world is contrasted with the boundless joy and peace that accompany the realization of one's spiritual nature

The second part of the chapter explores the themes of love and inner peace. It distinguishes between conditional and unconditional love, emphasizing that true love doesn't require a reason and is embodied as a lifestyle. The frequency of love and inner peace is portrayed as a shift in perception, where everything is seen through the lens of divine love, leading to a transformed experience of reality.

POINTS TO REMEMBER

✓ Spiritual Reality and Identity: Acknowledge consciousness as the true Self and embrace spiritual reality for true freedom and lasting happiness.

✓ Power of Belief: Recognize the influence of belief and faith on our experience of reality, as demonstrated by the placebo effect.

✓ Unconditional Love: Move beyond conditional love to unconditional love, seeing all existence as divinely perfect and lovable.

✓ Shift in Perception: Experience a shift in perception through the frequency of love, where everything is perceived with gratitude, purpose, and synchronicity.

✓ Acceptance of Spiritual Context: Understand that the true Self exists beyond the ego's attachment to the external world, bringing forth love, peace, and a sense of purpose.

JOURNALLING PROMPTS

Reflect on a moment when belief or faith significantly influenced your perception or experience of reality.

❧ JOURNALLING PROMPTS ❧

Explore your understanding of unconditional love. How can
you extend love beyond conditions and preferences?

_____

_____

_____

_____

_____

_____

_____

_____

_____

_____

_____

_____

_____

_____

_____

_____

_____

_____

_____

_____

_____

_____

_____

_____

☙ JOURNALLING PROMPTS ☙

Describe an experience where a shift in perception led to a deeper sense of gratitude and purpose in your life.

☙ JOURNALLING PROMPTS ☙

Consider a challenging situation and reflect on how viewing it through the lens of love might change your perspective.

✼ JOURNALLING PROMPTS ✼

Write about a belief system you hold that contributes to your sense of identity. How might loosening this attachment bring greater freedom and happiness?

☙ JOURNALLING PROMPTS ❧

Develop a daily practice to connect with your spiritual essence. This could be through meditation, prayer, or moments of mindfulness. Record your experiences and insights.

❧ JOURNALLING PROMPTS ❧

Contemplate your relationship with the fear of the unknown and death. How might embracing a spiritual context of reality alleviate these fears?

JOURNALLING PROMPTS

Reflect on instances where your experience of love was conditional. How did this impact your relationships and well-being? What steps can you take to move towards unconditional love?

_____

_____

_____

_____

_____

_____

_____

_____

_____

_____

_____

_____

_____

_____

_____

_____

_____

_____

_____

_____

_____

_____

_____

_____

❀ JOURNALLING PROMPTS ❀

Identify specific moments in your life where you felt a profound sense of inner peace. What factors contributed to these moments, and how can you cultivate more of them?

❀ JOURNALLING PROMPTS ❀

Recall a time when your faith in something, whether spiritual or not, influenced a positive outcome. How did this experience shape your understanding of faith?

ACTION PLANS

Unconditional Love Practice

Engage in a daily practice of expressing unconditional love. Choose specific moments to respond with love regardless of external circumstances.

Shift in Perception Exercise

Select a familiar environment and consciously shift your perception to see it through the lens of love. Note any changes in your emotional experience.

Gratitude Journaling

Maintain a daily gratitude journal, focusing on aspects of your life that are lovable and perfect just as they are.

Meditation on Spiritual Identity

Practice a meditation that explores your spiritual identity beyond the ego. Reflect on the idea that consciousness is the true Self.

Self-Reflective Questions

How can I deepen my understanding of spiritual reality and its role in shaping my identity?

In what areas of my life do I find it challenging to extend unconditional love?

What are some practical steps I can take to shift my perception and see the world through the lens of divine love?

How does the concept of true freedom and lasting happiness resonate with my current beliefs about existence?

THOUGHTS AND REFLECTIONS

THOUGHTS AND REFLECTIONS

Final note

Congratulations on completing the workbook for "The Inner Work". We hope this transformative journey has provided you with valuable insights, self-discoveries, and a deeper connection to your spiritual essence.

Your commitment to this inner work is commendable, and we encourage you to continue embracing the path of self-discovery and personal growth. Remember, the journey within is ongoing, and each step you take contributes to your evolution.

If you found this workbook impactful, we invite you to share your thoughts through a review. Your feedback is invaluable, not only for us but for fellow seekers who may embark on this journey. Your words have the power to inspire and guide others on their path of self-discovery.

Explore more transformative workbooks and resources by Zenful Work. Visit our website and discover a variety of tools designed to support you on your journey toward a more mindful, purposeful, and fulfilling life.

Thank you for choosing our workbook. May your continued exploration of the inner realms bring you profound wisdom, lasting peace, and true fulfillment.

Made in the USA
Columbia, SC
13 July 2024